Middle Youth

Middle Youth

Morgan Bach

TE HERENGA WAKA
UNIVERSITY PRESS

Te Herenga Waka University Press
Victoria University of Wellington
PO Box 600 Wellington
teherengawakapress.co.nz

A catalogue record is available at the National Library of New Zealand

ISBN 9781776920815

Printed in Singapore by Markono Print Media Pte Ltd

for Marian

Contents

III: to proceed within a trap

I

alone, lonely, or single

the pomegranate

you live in an open-air museum
where everyone is relaxing
into their graves

you walk through the heat
in olive groves, through the sound
of fountains, the stifling plain

baking late into the year,
you walk up hills to see mountains,
snow even, on the horizon

you are in doubt
when replying to locals
if the word you use means

alone, lonely, or single—but anyway
you make them laugh

you see the dust and orderly
bushes looking like polka dots
on tiered souvenir skirts

you sit in the window
above the street, feel the language
of passers-by lift up and strip you

you fuck the artist who says
he only collaborates
who then draws you at dinner

as hair around a blank oval, saying
the face doesn't matter

you hear the call echoing
on white walls, and bells on slick
marble outside the cathedral

your heart sinking in that basin
so picturesque you have to look
past it to the sierra, have to climb

to the top of the city to drink
mountain water from the fountain
behind the church

hungry

I always eat
the apple core.
To eat the sprouts
of plants is to eat potential
energy, the life force
of babies. Fill me
with the earth's iron,
I would drink
magma if I could.
One day, when my
insides are made
of steel, I will.
My oesophagus
a mine
of solid rock.
My spine
a skyscraper.
Heart an engine
of bolts and pistons.
Blood,
oil piped
from under ice
and all that
wind and water
will not
touch me.

red lake

For days we cross the highest plane.
I think of sea borders far from these stretches
of dust. This country's edge invisible as a trip line
or culture—a snag, a sudden immersion.

I long for a river to swim in
but we pass quickly into night with a crackle
of water-like light sliding over rocks
the sandy colour of peeled peaches.

By morning, my wet clothes hung to dry
in the window have frozen solid. The women
in my room have fine rivulets of blood running
from the softly steaming heat of their breath.

My cold skin is translucent; a blue hue in it
could be the stain of movement or a bruise.
Still it's home to me, like the remembered burn
and tickle of dusty carpet in sun, small mammal

howls, a forest along the sill, a window
to sit in. Framing is everything,
is the paint on my nails, turning feet from slugs
to sirens and the maraca

of my pulse, the invisible line behind me
and that wide red lake turning into sky
as birds rise and I part these rows
of bones to tell someone where I'm from.

blood moon

We are suspended in a forest of glass
and tonight the blood moon of earth
shuffling its shadow into the beam. Imagine
damming light—to hold it back, then burst.
What calculated magic we do
every time we flick a switch.
In our parcel of furnished air,
which window will show you
the moon's red light, symbol of what?
Of holding back? Tonight, bodies
obscuring light, our shadows warring
on the bedroom wall. When you move
away, I am blinded
and I rise, to turn off the flood.

clouds

roll,
south of the volcanoes.

You cut mushroom gills
soft as moth wings—

that fluttering in the belly.
Bread rising on the water tank.

Look out to patchy light
on the hills—moving.

Try to forget the names
of everything and call

them out new like rain
dropping on lava.

Steam born and gone in the same
instant. A thought of one

you still look up to see
isn't there.

terrific

Terrific as one who has their spine
set in the earth, who senses lucent
warmth coming in sideways, moves
in micro towards it. Who wants to feel light
like the soft skin of the water
before sinking in.

I salt my food to a point
almost unbearable to make
my blood buoyant.

I look for balance to the red interiors
in a calm sea of grasses, in the dull love
of dust on a hillside, in the caress of each
muscle as it contracts and expands
to pull me to a summit. That place
I would refuse to leave if I could,
but the hours have me by the ankles.

What I'm scared of is the pain of absence,
of nothing to fill my lungs. The space
outside that thin layer enclosing life.
The dark matter, untouchable,
the unknowable life in it.
How it might rise through our bodies
the higher we climb. I keep
waiting for the plague.

hoard

I cannot love you when the high street
smells of meat and metal, of almost-snow.

I spend my time with eyes
on a curvature never stepped to.

Some northern blood still running
warns of phone contracts,

leases and term deposits, loves
ribs of curved wood and bodies

of water, looks to crows
in their high nests

made stark in the rampikes of this stripped
land, cries promises to hoard change

and to hold it up like a compass
as soon as the green appears.

some bone

to S

They're a different kind of foreign to me,
as they were to you. Similar, but small
differences, like a bucket in the sink—
not enough to bail out of the habit of stating
things without hesitancy. Rolling vowels
like a colt on spring grass. Such confidence
in empire. Where you're stuck now
well above the flood, a whirling
washing line like I'd find at home
is just over the fence in your line of sight
(it's not—it's the sky) and a dog
that won't stop barking. Is it lazy to say
no one can work out what it's trying
to convey, how there is humour
in its aggression? I'll say it anyway.

because I

Because I say there is a hawk
they say there is not a hawk
it is too small, it does not prey

Because I know the path
they say it is not the path
and consult the satellites

Because I have been pierced
to make me safe from harm
they say it is not possible to defer vulnerability

Because I have seen the place in the north
they say maybe it is there, and doubt
that my eyes are also matter

that they see the path steepening
toward its edge, that they see
how the hawk does not care.

black hole

With every breath
we expel a pollen of thoughts.

Our hayfever minds, incendiary.
Syllables of stone around your ankles.

How can we live without
the consonant flight,

last touch of sun on peppery
flowers and an infinite universe.

We have microcosms in our chests.
Spit them out or feel them burst

and black holes, seeds failing to germinate,
will weigh your tongue back to soil.

Pluto

I scrolled through the day as a stream of pictures,
a receding track watched from the window,
hollow as the space traversed by Pluto, that totem
of the demoted, thumbing its way through silence.

To have been thought of as a planet doesn't change
how you see yourself. But to those who seemed to see
what you were and loved you for it, that lack
now the cause—feeling evaporating

beyond the warmth of rays, beyond the warmth
of another's thoughts. Removal of status,
just a big rock moving on your own orbit,
catching glimpses as you overlap in circular time.

The theoretical heart, size of a sweet mango, cradled in me—
it helped to think of it as abstract, folded away by a repetition
of men, a little drier each time, good with citrus
and chilli, growing sharp.

In photographs I looked restless, clothes rippled
by wind, legs braced on that dark track
through night, stroking the sheets
like they might rise up around me like a mouth.

oracle

just be smoke
that's a legacy
to leave behind

don't die in winter, imagine
no green
in the last view

we are stitches
a stitch, a stitch
I am the hem

let me explain, my sexuality
is that I would have made
a good oracle

I would take
or leave you after
cryptic truth, wordless

or brimming over, you mean
nothing or are prophecy
there is no middle ground

moderate fantasy threat

Sifting my skin through the millions of men
afloat in the city, their bodies barging like logs
on the stream of us, drifting in an intimate
disconnect, minds split like a coelenterate's.

I gather icons to flick through them like cards,
matchbooks gathering in the bottom of a bag, lie
to strike before them as though prostrated
at the altar of boredom, sex has become

an administrative task, instinct an appointment, a tally
against age, a weary American listing her lovers in a nineties
English romcom, oh I'm too old to be an ingénue in lust
with everyone. The movie of my life will be rated

with a certificate of moderate fantasy threat,
perhaps some bloody scenes to come.

I could love you for a moment
but there is democracy
to think of

the dark
is no longer
dark
but spotted
in gold
like the hide
of a cheetah
fast approaching

sometimes
your breath
smells like smoke
when you
wake

the sea in ribbons
of current
tangling as so many
snakes
in a nest

all day the ships
come and go
behind the burnt
pavilion

I wake
hungover
from sleep
I am the wall
your heart
cannot
leap

kelp and I
move
like we are kin

when I enter
the bush now
I am blind
a catalogue
of flowers
in my brain
I fear
will fade

one day
we won't know
what seasons
meant

already
winter
is not
winter

the snow
hushing
us to sleep
in spring

magpies

I like my lovers to tell me facts,
science, history, things I don't yet know,
so that when I am alone, listening to podcasts

in the bath has the same effect as company.
Hot water like a hug and the steam
of information, curated and saturating.

Dear magpies, bring me small facts
of affection, tokens of the world, ideas that prove
your love of it and, by extension, me.

The last few years, the ease of the cloister.
Unsought, enclosing. Patterns have become a choice,
the eddies of the mind an event horizon

in a world where each contact, each breath
could reach across distance to undo. But one touch
is a breeze across the water, a forked charge

grounding on the cold skinned sea. All kinds of hunger
tamped down by headlines and solitude.
Sometimes I think of a future

in which we've come through.
Saved, our expected disasters a bad memory
of collective night terrors—we'd been awake

but helpless. What will we do without our fear?
How will we frame ourselves if everything is in fact okay?
More likely the wind howling

through banks of the things we have been unable
to unsubscribe from. The tide of information
gathered without love, using up power.

The cloud beyond us. The cloud
a vast warehouse of servers in a stolen desert,
getting drier and drier.

The humming of air con
keeping our unwanted thoughts
just below combustion point.

date line

On Dreadnought Walk
the box hedge smells
of piss, children

playing by the river.
You are no one's mother
and you are running.

How many dogs today
have crossed
the meridian line?

No one has ever
loved you like
a location,

London gaslit blue
by the underside
of towering cloud.

The city has doubled
down on your luck,
delivered an incompetent grope

in a Wapping alleyway.
Towers lit like lamps,
a businessman's burning fingers

in you at Canary Wharf.
A cinematographer, a prophetic
hedge maze at Crystal Palace

you could both see over,
exit visible by the second bend.
The anxious sibling

of a famous actress.
Another, slowly going blind,
who took you to the bar

the Krays shot up.
A surgeon whose hands
would open you decisively,

in correction or want.
All simply there while the backdrop
lapped at your heart.

Another date, another line
you found yourself crossing,
committing to the tide.

You walk through churches you don't believe in
with your body
you don't believe in.

You came back because
you had been exquisitely lonely
here, once before

and unresolved
loneliness is an unresolved
triumph, and failure

a comfort, a career
spinster under the knife
of indifferent hands.

The horrific river,
the date line,
the tidal surge.

II

middle youth

ichthyic

I have swum in many seas
but it's never enough.
There is always so much more water
rising to form new bodies.

Lost inland seas, deserts, hexagonally tiled salt flats,
these are the places my heart quickens, here I see
no hands of gods, just the chemical bones of suns,
matter pooled brine-like in all of us still living.

I would swim in the past, be a seed
in the salinity of the world. That ancient sea,
long buried or raised to dry, from which we grew
our first greed, and crawled out, and went forth to claim everything.

carousel

orange blossom, an olfactory
loneliness on the brittle street

pang to avenues of green
an ink of weeds to mark

the skin, to hold its betrayals
to perform them in nervous carousel

*

at work my favourite bird walks three steps
to scream at the ground, and then again

at night I am the reluctant sniper, the hawk,
I determine who rises from the field

at night a different life where I fly
to perch beside mosaics of a mother

and baby, adult-eyed god, fall to
nightmares of birds I've caged

*

the violence done to the minds
and bodies of our mothers,

before our time, works like a glacier
moving slowly on our selves

*

but now, having swallowed full moons
coupled with mirrors of reticence, I find

life is not an experiment like that
and soon the body gives up its hunt

how soon the body becomes a cliff
how soon the body becomes a full stop

while you keep on moving in it

after Sissinghurst

for H.H.

Plants stacked in a green library of messages
we falter now to read, seeing decoration
flattened without the symbolic.
How deeply the sun lifted crimson
to our surfaces, in June, in the north
and what that meant to us now,
a rolling black sand beach, a skipping
heartbeat, a revolving burden. A making
of oneself into an emotional zebra skin,
distinct, warring, a whole.

To have hands all day in soil and sap
and all night in words and lovers,
that is the life we want, that we can
no longer pay for.

To think the perfect English garden was a
camouflage, an expression of those that would be
ostracised—every plotted cliché is built
on a slanted mirror after all, a slick-surfaced
pond, teeming fish circling near the steps
for a delivery or disturbance
to the surface.

To be left alone with a garden,
to be given love in a garden,
to be given love at all, and to leave
your meadows unmown and full of life,
adders content in the undergrowth.

Make my canon of wildflowers and edible
trees, I see now how your woods are not
a dull wall of bright green
but all woven of shapes and shades and
softness, bound with burrs.

Ten-foot perennial, pale sun, silver thistle,
a strawberry leaf with organ-red flowers,
you should always have to rise
from a garden in order to write, ascend
a spiral staircase into the rising night,
turning into an orb-like room
that exists unaware of direction, that follows
its own course above perfection, above
the white garden, from where you can see
the colour sneaking in.

turning, hurtling

I march diligently
to sunshine in the park

everything bathed
and turning golden.

A woman breathes fire
by the folly framing her

like a personal door to hell.
Conkers are pitched from high boughs

to break and give up fruit, a spire
emergent from the baring trees

the endless rustle of blackbirds
searching in detritus underfoot.

Autumn is a loud season.
Through the wall the neighbour cries

no, no, then yes. I am a constant ache
where I hinge. I'm unsure

what season my body is in,
losing the hours, thinking to deadline.

Already I crave new foliage,
my will browning round the edges.

I must become a self-sustaining
ecosystem. Must rebuild dams

to equalise my impulses,
must hope there is something living

back there in the hills, and running.
Must prepare for the conditions by which

when winter comes
I will step on to the ice.

*

I gather with friends and strangers
in the long grass of the heath

bottles of fizz in our coat pockets.
The city offers something to compensate us

for our empty fear, to placate us
and the plague-dead we stand upon.

There's no unburdened ground.
We murmur, reduced to pre-verbal excitement

nerves licked by the smell of gun powder,
sparks collapsing back on you.

Delight in mass dumbness,
at bursting thistles and silver jellyfish rain

screeching ghoul-whirlers like enraged sperm
shot into the sky. Yes little atoms it is right

to hurtle into the future screaming,
to cry at the unknown.

The tornado of stasis I feel
facing loss upon loss. To burn things

to gather in fields and burn things,
to in our thousands ignite it all

not for the failure
but for the attempt.

For days the dark is filled with booming
and peripheral glimpses of fire.

(an administrative poem)

The allergen presents in slow-growing manifestations,
a threat by increase, a tolerance drop. Your skin bubbles

out of nowhere, as though you're boiling alive. An allergy
can be emotional, as in I am allergic to the presentation

of your entitlement into my personal ecosystem, as in I am
allergic to the scrutiny you couple with instructive realities

only you can see the horizon of, as in I am bubbling,
turning inside out with this moving around of paper

and next time I react it may be
that I cannot breathe.

cosmos

vacuum decay

I wake in the low hours,
thighs and small of back
alight from inside, cramps
like a sunburn without heat.

I have been reading theories
about the universe's end
and this one might come
to fruition. My particles evaporating

from the pure vacuum inside me,
bubbling out to ruin everything.
In Iceland, people have gathered
to watch fire pouring from a fissure

sprung in rock. Its new cone
as perfect as a science fair replica
collapses on one side, an under-baked cake.
What appeared solid remains molten.

The spectators run for higher ground
and I wonder if it will reach them, encase and cool
to ashy hollows. But it's too slow.
Life is only moving as fast as I feel it.

bounce

We have moved to cities with different patterns
in the footpaths, drifting out as the space
between now and our childhoods grows deeper.
We spread into our lives, occupy wooden floors, kitset desks,

the small rooms of other people's hearts.
We consume—the miles walked in foreign countries,
the crops of a failing globe. The energy it takes
to be a person, we can't sustain it,

will peak and condense to our first selves,
the old friends of our smaller lives
where we began, where we bounced
everything off each other.

big rip

I am not great
at constants, usually trying
to get away, never quite
unpacked.

One day I might outrun
myself, force
my own unravelling.
My rip-a-stitch longings

for the edges of things,
what hasn't been seen.
What is a self but a place
to journey outwards from?

Each field is an expansion,
the turquoise and orange sky
clashing at dusk, always something brighter
over the horizon.

heat death

We want, we want
more.
It just goes on.
The river moving

always away, gathering
itself as it goes,
chaotic, replenishing
from a dark singularity.

Can anything stay
held together? Within weeks
my skin is dust on the shelves
of my new room.

Every book I read takes me
further from the first narrative,
coats me as I coat it with old cells,
leaves me richer and emptier.

Where does the river end?
When it becomes the sea.
And does the sea know itself
as many drops of river?

big crunch

We know our luck
is borrowed
from our future selves.
Each time we make it home

could be the last time.
Tentative in our walking out,
building worlds around ourselves
where we are allowed

to simply walk, alone.
The street lights on this road
out to the valley hide stars,
their pasts bright against the dark.

If I cross to the unlit side,
I'll see them, stop scanning the road
to let my eyes focus. Look out
past the fear that something

will turn back on you, a volatile
energy might storm in upon us,
condense to nightmare,
a van, a hand on arm, tightening.

realised fears

That my instinct might not make up
for learning, the lack of natural
skill, my friends racing ahead
on longer legs, their grammar
inherent, while I brash on
into obscurity. I'm not good
with people or with words
and what else is there to tally
against love, against lovableness—
no rewards for sitting quietly,
for being minerals in space.
You have to have a will to impose,
but if you do it might be gaudy.
You have to love the right open spaces,
the ones allowed into your cells.
There are rules about everything,
about what's cool, and caring isn't,
but I've always had the wrong kind
of detachment, the kind no one
wants to overcome. I am thinking
of cutting my hair off, the way Hana does
when they get to the monastery
before she piles books into stairs,
before she knows she will open
again, despite herself, to diffusion.

pasture

South of the sea road, in winter,
the hills, folded tight as bundled cloth,
appear lit from within when the sun breaks
over the eastern range.

These hills don't raise the eyes
of most in this train carriage, don't pull
like the view over sea and islands do—they gather in,
they oppose a sense of distance.

So bare, like the intimate places of other bodies.
I cannot pass them without taking in
their bright pasture. I graze on them.
This stretch of un-wild green,

transposed from ideas of other countries,
stays clipped and worked, moulded like a colonial batter.
Is it beautiful in the way a desert is beautiful? Changed
from its old life as ocean or prairie.

On other spines of the coast pasture is giving way,
reverting to scrubby bush, seedlings, nursery cover.
In my lifetime I could see new canopy, hopeful
in the way a woman just past 'her peak',

feeling the prickling freedom of not giving a fuck,
glows with that new power—of those that have been put
out to pasture in the minds of men, who in all our lifetimes
have been the ones to decide.

I raise my eyes to look at them. The common sight
of farmland in this country,
stripped, loaded with destructive history,
regenerating, growing in the tightest seams.

fury

She would teach them how to limpet
to nothing but the arc of the sun,
its coursing arm around their shoulders
in the dark cinema of their futures.

She would grant them lust
like a charm when the fire gas
was falling on a green battlefield
where no one was the enemy.

She would push them into the mud,
their decorum lost to a fever,
release the gate of their pop song
hearts and she the cold cup and the whip.

When she took delivery of them,
arriving stretchered, prone,
back to her care, the best medicine
was always to sing them into letting go.

gravity

Late autumn. The birds are chasing olives
down the street, small winged anti-Sisyphus
intent on a feast. There seems purpose to the smallest action
of birds, they way they look you in the eye when landing
on the letterbox, drop a white shit while meeting your gaze.
They don't care about you. Though they spend a lot of time
flying from point to point with no measurable
outcome, I have faith in their inherent magnetic sense
of the curve below them as they rise, that they know
gravity as a marble of rest, a sphere pulling
at the poles, that point to point is always home.

Thursday

Thursday, because there is shouting
that's not in the film. Out back, the concrete
square that equals my gratitude
bouncing voices from the neighbourhood,
horns, spatulas on pots, some kind of trumpet,
confused birds at dusk. We are not sure why
this is life now but we commit.

London still averts its eyes
as the tide rises, as we leave
Europe for dust. I run because
it is a treat to be embodied in the outdoors.
The southeastern keeps its timetable
running past my bedroom window. Somewhere
those empty carriages meet the sea.

Pleasure in drying rounds of washing on the line,
a flight of stairs to walk up, the trees first
in lime bright leaf and then in flower,
in how they sting the eyes, in rain
which rinses the streets of people
and the fear of being overwhelmed.
I joke with the stranded, we'll steal

a ship and sail home, conditioned to cabin life.
Revise a ritual of return, my childhood of counting
loops of the backyard, naming the towns
from Te Kūiti to Wellington. Always homesick
for somewhere I'm not and somewhere I am.
Now I loop the sanctuary of Greenwich Park and allow myself
to imagine the quick way, count it, the miles

converting back to metric, that's London
Bridge at the beech, the hawthorn hedge
of Heathrow, double back for the long aerial sweep
to the humid halfway of the azalea glade,
full loops over oceans, a few more for good
measure before the coastline appears
in the oval portal of my longing.

But I turn the key to the same door
as yesterday, which was a week, a month of Thursdays,
and there is my friend calling with a digital birdsong, saying
it's almost time to dance and in her living room
a day ahead of me she has started
and in the background I can hear
her daughter saying, 'No, Mummy, no stop, it's horrible.'

middle youth

I can never say to my friends with newborns
I am afraid.
They have taken on our failure,
made it personal.

I'm already so tired I can feel
my heart beating.
Feel it trying to keep up
with everything.

When I had the virus it was there, beating
like a faint
drum of war. Another
pep talk to myself.

Though all our parents still
feel like teenagers
they are slowing as though a wind
drags on them.

I've lost at least a decade somehow.
The days added
up to more than I can believe.
All those hours lost

to sleep, all those beats lost
to disgust
at selves we'd gladly take back,
those missing friends.

This clutch of years made a few
decisions for me,
world events an aid
to resolution.

No children, a definition
of home, who one should be
in a time zone with
even when the days stretch out

into a rainless plain
of your own company.

*

We all went to see Hilma.
The spinsters, thornbacks, the bubble
of our demographic.
What plucks at me

is not her language of symbols
or words of instinct but the way
The Ten Largest marched the long wall,
childhood so quickly giving way

to youth, slipping to the adult
which stretches the length of the gallery
till the final orderly panel
of old age.

Like a weekend with no variation, no crumbling
pegs to clip activities to, the years of this

middle youth
both stretch out and flee behind you.

The days clutter with memes of the events
we've seen, a millennial history
of disaster, our xennial cringe—we anger
that we have become, suddenly,

the adults.
That the long gallery ahead might not be hung
with pastels, flower forms, with covetable
images of security,

with flourishing, communion.
Every human who lived on this planet
has feared one future or other
but the gallery

is dimming the lights
for closing
the paintings ahead getting harder
to see—no children.

I could find a nicer way to say it
but when skinned
that's what my own fear means.
There will be no children.

In most other years I'd be dead by now.
The drum keeps on beating,
in theory
there is still a lot left.

If you have children, you are expecting
someone to outlive you.
I can't quite look at this even as the minutes
call its past tense into existence. I water

my plants, throw seeds to sparrows,
focus on the painting in front of me,
a middle kind of year
in which far too much and nothing has happened.

*

My mother says I'm becoming quite
domesticated, because I bought a reading lamp
and some cushions. I'm almost
forty and just trying

to feel respectable, accept some comforts,
furnish my den with the symbolic
language of control. I walk to work
through the park, eye drawn

through the saplings to a shelter
of branches and pine needles.
In this market a single person's retirement plan
can look like anything.

Hard not to want to retire immediately
when we don't know if we will reach
retirement. After work
I walk up hills—am always happier

going up. Something like loss
in every turning back.
The room of the gallery we've just left
was always flooding,

the too much of our youths
still seeping towards our feet,
ghost selves lapping.
The sun is full out

and we're still dewy.
The desiccating is just a distant light.
Still taking every vaccine I can,
paying into the pension scheme.

Every year the high
water mark
a little higher.
We are always happier going up.

blood and sand

A suitable drink for a coven
now we've stumbled upon it.
The human menu was a knot
of fine strings, flavours
we have had to tease out of her
as though finding an elixir
to soften the edges of this inherited
mess is indeed magical. We are soothed
by our discovery, this tulip

of dusty red. Named not,
as we all assumed, for a woman
near water, but for a hero of blood sports,
of ending things in gore and glory.
We, conversely, are trying to keep
ourselves and others alive, are still
surprised to have made it so far as
to be unsure of the birthday
we are celebrating.

Earlier, I was trying to explain myself to a man
I used to love, and still do in a wary
and more temperate way. To explain the hesitance
I've tangled myself in, dehydrating in a trap
of distorted electrical impulses. It always goes wrong,
the explanation goes off course like a river bursting its banks,
the vulnerability I held back too long.
What feels desperately true isn't enough,
just seeps away into the sand.

I've tried to love in the way
we are conditioned to believe
essential to human experience—
a measure of fullness, inherent goodness,
marking a person of sufficient quality.
But what are human qualities anyway? And where
should I find them in myself? The top shelf
of my personality, the shaker that
no longer quite seals.

The barman sparks a flint
into our glasses. Will we taste
the extinguished flame?
Vulnerability steamed off, leaving
smoky fruit on the palate, a hint of fire,
words pouring out, soaking
into the silence of an unread message,
a reaching out
with the rags of your fine red flag.

III

to proceed within a trap

Venus

In the polar blast of our hottest June
a sudden rekindling of feeling
for the evening star, drawing
new probes—multiple ventures—to its broiling
surface. Love-struck planet,
guiding light, false fire hovering
on the horizon.

The almost twin, the sibling
who didn't fear getting closer
to the sun, that brave
vision of hell. But could it,
they wondered, have once
been oceanic—been a bearer
of life? Perhaps it is normal

in this orbit, to trigger
events, to lure a runaway
into spiralling sulphuric clouds,
fracture and volcanoes, a trampoline
of heat in an atmosphere where oceans
long burned out, or is it unlucky?
Astounding, how little we know.

to proceed within a trap (i)

Make your tent a chlorophyll skin.
Make your tent your skin.

Sit by every round window you come upon.
Devise seas inside yourself.

Pay no heed to divisions of the year. All calendars are steps
to the platform at the top of a temple. All temples fall.

Listen to the rhythm beaten out by hares and when they run,
remain as a landmark in the rain.

No Spitfire can turn like a meadowlark. No lark
will burn like a Spitfire over the cliffs.

Imagine those you could love.
Imagine those who will forgive you.

Some seeds sit dormant, some
viruses too.

It is a cruelty that womb
and tomb rhyme, and at times collide.

How many bends in the road can you bear
to see.

We have been scribing for millennia, we have scribbled all over
everything but we are not satisfied.

After all this time, ink
still has to dry.

Hide your hated selves between leaves
in the library, where they will not feel alone.

It will seem obvious, and then you will find
you have forgotten.

You have forgotten the smell
of snow after the soot is covered.

You have forgotten that none of this
was requested, and yet was given.

All you have to do is proceed,
and know, and do it anyway.

Blönduós

for M.W.

Relief, that the taps in the church
also run sulphuric

> both terminals of the arch of judgement
> perhaps smell the same

>> from the cracked but clear
>> bell tower window beside the bath

>> the sea
>> Húnafjörður

all other glass is coloured
and turns you inward

> Early spring there were seals
> out in the surf

> before the ice melted
> into a slurry at the river mouth

> before night
> retreated to its very edges

>> that insomniac sun
>> you bargain with as it dips

>> below the sea's far lip
>> and make plans for morning

and when shortly after
the ever light gets lighter

you find you are
already there

to proceed within a trap (ii)

To proceed within a trap,
give up your house and lover
for a barely ex war zone,

run in the compound, armour
under suit, at weekends drink
with other hyper-responsible

runaways. Or merely continue
as I do, on your odd commute
to avoid any output

not determined by meetings
or global politics. Yes we could
adopt a teenager but we would be

a circus act of self-loathing
and never have another holiday
greater than taking off our glasses

and enjoying the blur.

p is for pterodactyl

Zaiga knows that p is for pterodactyl
which is also what we call the kākā now shrieking
above the city at dusk, riding vents
over Wellington's high valleys,
making use, finally, of those last pines
that we are surely waiting to see die
or be cut out.

I know that she, like other small humans,
loves dinosaurs and so I buy her
dino stencils for Christmas
so she can repopulate
the earth with their shapes,
the spines and necks we can identify
as though we've been keeping
an eye out all this time. What rustles
behind that fern? Terrible short arms?

I can't remember the point
of knowing. That these wondrous beasts
were not fantasy, or rare creatures
from elsewhere in place. That it was a question
of elsewhere in time. That over
and over there is a clear-out,
a planetary garage sale, a flash
flood of extinctions.

The scaly, cuddly comfort, the animated
ghosts of the earth, are everywhere.
We paper our children's walls

with mascots of catastrophe.
Bedspreads, soft toys, patterned T-shirts,
dinosaur onesies to embrace our young
in this symbol, this irony. We love
what we can never encounter,
while we are young.

And when we realise, it's too late to see
what has been lost.

To proceed within a trap (iii)

It used to be that we would imagine our older years
in comfort, longing to be looked after again.

Now that seems like a medieval
miracle play, actors booming

proclamations, reassurances
we don't believe will come to pass.

When I used to feel earthquakes
they were the land

grinding, creaking like a house
in the wind. We were always jumping

under door frames, eyes round as the cat's
on fireworks night.

Now I feel them, and I go still,
look to the ceiling for a drunken lamp,

realise it is just my body,
my own pulse quaking,

my heart suddenly aware
of its clenching,

surging blood through its ribbons and meat,
self-directed

and shaking me
like a disaster.

*

My dreams used to be wild
and played across great expanses.

Gone is Bear Mountain, the swooping
flights over desert cities

the ever expanding house
of my inner self

where new rooms would appear
like crocuses in the grass.

Now the road crumbles under me,
the path turns to cliff

and I must fly through a web of wires, sparking
to fill the sky like contrived lightning.

There are no secret rooms,
there is no house,

it burned up
years ago.

*

How often do we realise something is missing
only when we hear it again?

The hum of summers in our childhoods,
bees so numerous you would hesitate

to walk across a lawn
spotted with clover.

I heard it, that buzz, deep
in its collective, the haste of pollen.

I was standing on the ruin
of a city

five millennia old and it sounded
like summer in the 1980s.

In the scheme of 'us', our brief burst
of time, those epochs

lay side by side. That hum
lit up its decades of decline,

its absence
from our ears.

Under the city, on a path like a paved
gorge, I walked into the silence

of a hive-shaped tomb.
The bones of its human queen

long gone, a chamber now
in which to test our own echoes.

*

When I heard the seedbank
had sprung a leak,

I felt doom cutting the ribbon
like a politician

leaking secrets
of the state we're in.

Permafrost melting, trickling into the tunnel
carved sloping into the bedrock.

Oh they say it's fully waterproof
now, designed for a 'virtually infinite lifetime'.

We should know better
than to hope in the past, to pretend

we are ever at base level.
Everything is floating on a fictional line.

Each day I swim a little further out,
ride the deep lip of water,

the darkening slope of the caldera
dropping away below.

*

Ophiojura: brittle star,
180 million years a genetic loner.

Eight jaws, microscopic teeth bundled
like the needle-thin hair of a cactus

in each crevice of a mouth
at the star's centre.

Limbs like ropes anchoring
to their deep-sea mountain.

To survive is perhaps dependant
on not wanting much,

not aspiring to move beyond your natural
habitat, having an excess of teeth.

*

Another decade has passed in limbo,
a maze of small choices.

We shuffle always onwards
through the trap.

Events flood from the radio,
though time feels fictive:

all is still while we hurtle.
I remain on my underwater mountain,

my volcanic patience spilling ash
into the brine of my half-woken day.

There isn't going to be a thread
to lead us back out

to the world we remember.
Those people we were then

are gone. Their world
by degrees hotter,

quieter
in summer.

sweet spot

Everyone's favourite father
was Cosby.

We could all be anything we wanted—
thousands of prime ministers.

Molly could Frankenstein a ball dress
out of her dead mother's clothes

and become the coolest
girl in school.

We watched action movies,
each explosion just a thrill—

fossil fuels were burning anyway,
open oil fires in the Middle East,

unquestionable wars, the wall
down, the market always open,

fast-food birthdays, cartoon figurines
to collect with the produce

of new Amazonian farmland. We worried
about atolls but also how many things

we got for Christmas, which plastic
approximation of a colonised princess.

Suburban jeeps meant an Indiana Jones
lived next door, small-town builder

with a swimming pool, heated
against the open air,

electricity endless, the summer warm
but droughtless, grass always green

everywhere. A pet lamb to raise
and never ask after

when it disappeared.

to proceed within a trap (iv)

The world is still full of great men
making it completely unliveable for the rest of us.

I've never hatched anything,
never hatched a plan,

never laid out any human interventions
in the future.

In late-stage capitalism
everything is strung with fairy lights.

Every revolution needs bunting
to declare a position—,

beads of electrons
as numerous and trapped as we are.

I've stopped taking photographs
of anything but water,

my back to the neon writing that scrolls the stock
exchange held above the lost swamp.

Our economic positions figured
with accepted wisdom of great men.

Fake flowers suddenly seem
an ecological stance,

as rivers dry up—
soon even Hollywood will be on fire.

We were coloured in by the loves
of great men, babysat

by romcoms and fantasy affluence.
But California is burning—

the mountain ridges shrivelled
like cellulose stalled

and combusting behind the projector light.
Ah but it's all digital now, fake negatives,

pixels are the ecological choice
for water usage.

What of small outposts,
the shadow towns of cinema—

Miramar readying itself
to become a lake.

So many sets built, past, future, other
worlds in the landfill.

*

I work the bar at the book launch
of a local hero's biography.

The great woman is dead
of course, like they all are.

I offer the finance minister a wine
so I can leave the tide out, in spite,

but he refuses me, my passive-aggressive note
on political timidity—

I'm longing for the socialist wonderland
they threatened.

My father and I give our bets
for the expiry of the species.

It's a fun new game we play,
a familial reckoning with despair.

His mother used to get the giggles
talking about death.

When I first heard this I assumed
it was a nervous reaction,

but maybe she just found it all
hilarious, a morbid riot of futility.

To escape war my grandfather drove
through the desert like he didn't care

if the sand sucked him under.
He saved my father's to-be-ness

and consequently mine.
I'd never meet my grandmother—

perhaps the joke she was getting,
as I walk through the world with her hair,

and wonder if it will lose its colour
before I'm swallowed.

We ride fast
through the wars of great men.

＊

I look, frankly, magical when bathed
in the distant light of a forest fire.

When Portugal smouldered,
the sky in London glowed like Campari

at 4 in the afternoon.
Friends photographed me pulsating

with the sugary dusted glow
of a redhead in apocalyptic light.

That's one thing I suppose
perhaps I'll hit peak attractiveness yet—

but who wants to be hot
on a doomed planet?

Can we laugh at this? Would it not
be better to rage? At finance ministers

drunk on figures, at every former hippy
who treats us like cultural vending machines

while they drink
our sweat for rent?

While they still treat this all
like theatre.

We fetch and serve, we trade
in imaginations, riffs and retellings,

because no one can imagine
the future anymore,

without laughing
like my grandmother—

her fast husband back from hell,
her hair aflame.

Oh we laugh
in the faces of great men,

while they watch us burn,
while they look at figures.

health & safety

My worst back injury came
from nothing. A twist in a cold room,
or bending to tuck in a sheet,
or reaching for shoelaces, or dreaming.
I straightened like a tendril,
weakest tender shoot of a vine
before walking.

Every year is a hundred year
according to the weather.
The seasons, a sign of health,
slip down the months like slurry
after a flood. The ooze
of unease, of hoarded wealth,
empty houses, the new feudal
system. Take comfort, that there are worse
years in the past, 536 when a great fog
hid the sun, or when ships came, flush
with pox in 1492.

My highest place is etched into me,
carried everywhere I go, now that I'm back
at sea level, and don't know if I'll travel again.
We were allowed to walk among the honeycomb
of boiling mud pools. Soft greys, warm belly fur
of the altiplano, sulphur adding flavour
to the altitudinal haze in our blood.
Unregulated health and safety
amazed me as I wove across
the rupturing field.

I once got to rise above the land.
Always fearing heights, being a person
whose brain spins into any open air
I thought I wouldn't hold my nerve
as the gas huffed fire into the silk.
The fabric filled with hot air like a pretty
bloated animal, not stricken and immobile,
but lifting into the cold dawn air.

When the roaring ascent was done
the sky was quiet.
My brain a silken valley of calm
so far below me,
a softly bending back,
a new world below.

to proceed within a trap (v)

I have watched that Beatles doco
and now I'm not sure what to do

with my life. The immediate hours
and the days that go on,

for now. I watched it with three
generations of family, my sister

our tired host, her kids' interest
fluctuating, our mother telling

everyone how old she was
at different points in their career.

I work out it's only thirteen years before
my birth that they're sitting

in a circle pulling songs
from somewhere, seemingly the air.

Weird to want to fill in the gaps
for them, they're so familiar.

My other sister keeps climbing hills,
getting to the top

and crying, she tells me.
She's not sure why, but it's nice

to get out of the too big house,
which is losing occupants

between each of my visits.
She's so young, there are so many

decisions, and Tinder is so grim.
We have a look through anyway.

I think everyone has had a hard year,
even though it's gone so fast

in its weirdness that even my nephews
feel it, their young years rushing.

And yet, I don't know what to do
with these last few weeks, before

the year turns. Certainly
I won't do anything world changing

or even life changing. I probably
won't encounter anyone

I don't already know, it's almost
the holidays after all

and we can't go anywhere. I will age,
the counting day is soon.

I'll try to be okay about it, feel lucky
it's happening at all.

Did the future always gape? An empty
room, requiring a rhythm, a melody

to appear from somewhere, the air to fill
with a scaffolding from out of the minds

of people with enough ego
to give the rest of us something

to look at, to sing along to. To fill
our hours, and our children's hours.

A little line of notes to chase
through these last few weeks

to the fresh silence
of a new year.

the museum of prophecies

Roof curved against the weight of snow,
a season I can still feel like a memory
on the landscape in late spring.
The sturdy resident priestess, in fleece
and the cropped hair of a woman with things to do,
draws the cards.

My first ever reading.
I like the idea of a narrative
to hang my uncertainties on.
Dagny, inheritor of the oracles,
last in a long line, turns the card
that tells her who I am: the High Priestess.

She eyes me. 'You're on your own path.'
A kind way of putting it, and not wrong
though the dog has been taking me for walks
all week, picked me straight off for someone
who will succumb, who will follow along.
One day we struck out for the hills,

the cliffs above the sea,
until she rebelled, turned decisively back
to the river, always the river
and the game of stones.
But here she is, the High Priestess,
the lonely path.

The Temperance card a warning tucked
into her side. Her future, a card that shows

things passing her by. The Five of Cups, she stands stuck
on a stone in the rushing river. Dagny gives me
a bald look, it is spring, she says,
and the waters are rising.

We drive across the country, my friends and I,
holding our new stories close. On my knee, the dog
steams up the windscreen with her hot breath.
On Hrísey, we circle the island
to a place said to be on ley lines.
The mountain across the fjord

directing energy down on us, three
depleted women, not really believing
anything but the thrill of a new story.
The dog lies down facing the mountain
and we wonder if she senses something
or is just tired from walking some of the way

through swampy ground. There seem very few
people here. The houses give off a pastoral gothic.
We sit by a small lake, eating sandwiches,
rolling over our stories
and when were aren't watching
the dog jumps in. The charged water

flying off her in sheets as she shakes.
The cards also told me of babies
and divorces, neither my own. Of family
reconciliations, of people coming to contentment.
I was given the Tower, a tumbling to come, a life
to rebuild from the foundations. The Lovers, tied

to work—a King of Cups I already knew.
Dagny thought it would work out.
The sky takes on a polar clarity,
day stretching at its edges.
On the way home we stop to soak
in a hot spring metres from the sea.

Everywhere is volcanic, all living things
clutching. We walk over a dune to the beach,
find a whale there, alone, its ribcage open to the air.

Notes

For more on the five theories referenced in 'cosmos' (p. 44), I'd recommend *The End of Everything: (Astrophysically Speaking)* by Katie Mack, which inspired this poem sequence, and manages to be accessible and funny despite its subject matter. Team vacuum decay, all the way.

The title 'To proceed within a trap' (p. 63) is borrowed from Karla Marchesi's series of paintings of the same name: karlamarchesi.com/galleries/2019/proceed-within-trap/ Karla, in turn, borrowed this title from a Syrian art film.

'Venus' (p. 65): Some phrases in this poem are borrowed from an article by Robin McKie, 'Why science can't resist the allure of Venus: New missions to Earth's nearest planetary neighbour', *Guardian*, 4 July 2021, theguardian.com/science/2021/jul/04/why-science-cant-resist-the-allure-of-venus-new-missions-to-earths-nearest-planetary-neighbour

'health & safety' (p. 86): You can read more on the grim events mentioned in this poem in the following articles.

Oliver Milman, 'European colonization of Americas killed so many it cooled Earth's climate', *Guardian*, 31 Jan 2019, theguardian.com/environment/2019/jan/31/european-colonization-of-americas-helped-cause-climate-change

Ann Gibbons, 'Why 536 was "the worst year to be alive"', *Science*, 15 Nov 2018, science.org/content/article/why-536-was-worst-year-be-alive

Acknowledgements

Earlier versions of some of these poems have been published in *Sport*, *Mimicry*, *JAAM*, *4th Floor Journal*, *Sweet Mammalian*, *Turbine | Kapohau*, *The Spinoff* and *Ōrongohau | Best New Zealand Poems*. Thank you to the editors.

Thank you to Karla for the use of your beautiful painting for the cover. (All of Karla Marchesi's work is incredible—go feast your eyes on it!) Massive thanks to THWUP: Fergus, Craig, Todd, Ebony and especially Ashleigh for her cheerleading, patience and fine editorial eye. The poems are much better for your polish and grasp on punctuation.

Thanks to my family, always. Thanks to the friends who are in the context of these poems, or sometimes actually in them, and to friends in my other hometown, London (I miss you), Aotearoa and elsewhere, and those who have been in writing groups with me over the last decade. I'm a very lucky person when it comes to friends, and I love you all. Particular thanks to Hannah: without our poetry pact and your encouragement I dunno if I'd ever have finished this one. Thanks to booksellers, especially at our indie bookstores! Fuck the internet, buy local! Booksellers are paid peanuts for their fierce general knowledge—you want them on your quiz teams and in your cities, trust me.

I have spent half the last decade living in London, and consequently a number of poems are set there, or in Spain, Greece, Iceland, etc. You could say that being Sagittarius sun AND moon explains the wanderlust, but really I've just been very privileged (I see it) to have had the opportunity to travel and I have spent every cent I've earned doing so. I may have to retire to a tent. And lastly, thanks to everyone who has endured my rambling about getting 'middle youth' into the vernacular. Still about twenty years till we are adults, people . . . the campaign continues!